A COMPLEX LANGUAGE

"The teams are at the *line of scrimmage*. The *center* snaps the ball to the *quarterback* who *fades back* to throw a *forward pass*. Wait—it's a *safety blitz*. The *passer* moves out of the *pocket* . . . he's being chased by the *free safety*. Now he *throws* a short pass to his *fullback* out in the *left flat*. The ball carrier picks up his *blockers*, and runs along the *sideline* for a *first down* before the *right linebacker* shoves him *out of bounds*. But I think there may be a *clipping penalty*. . . ."

Can you follow all the plays the sportscaster is describing? This cross-referenced dictionary gives you clear, simple explanations of football terms so you can understand the complexities of this exciting game.

FOOTBALL TALK

HOWARD LISS

AN ARCHWAY PAPERBACK
Published by POCKET BOOKS • NEW YORK

This book was originally published under the title *Football Talk for Beginners*.

 An Archway Paperback published by
POCKET BOOKS, a Simon & Schuster division of
GULF & WESTERN CORPORATION
1230 Avenue of the Americas, New York, N.Y. 10020

ISBN: 0-671-43472-1

First Pocket Books printing September, 1973

10   9   8   7

AN ARCHWAY PAPERBACK and colophon are
trademarks of Simon & Schuster.

Printed in the U.S.A.

IL 4+

FOOTBALL TALK

ABBREVIATIONS AND SYMBOLS USED IN DIAGRAMS

BH	BALL HOLDER	LLB	LEFT LINEBACKER
BL	BLOCKER	MLB	MIDDLE LINEBACKER
C	CENTER	OG	OFFENSIVE GUARD
DE	DEFENSIVE END	OT	OFFENSIVE TACKLE
DHB	DEFENSIVE HALFBACK	P	PUNTER
DT	DEFENSIVE TACKLE	QB	QUARTERBACK
FB	FULLBACK	RLB	RIGHT LINEBACKER
FLB	FLANKER BACK	S	SAFETY
HB	HALFBACK	SE	SPLIT END
K	KICKER	TE	TIGHT END

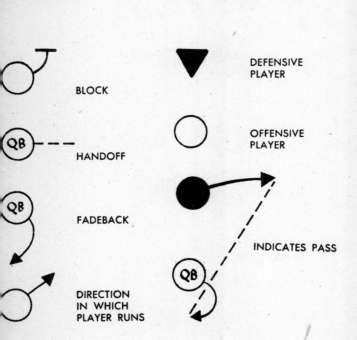

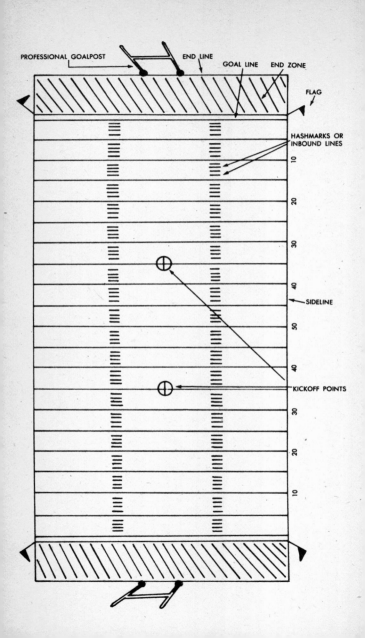

ALL-AMERICAN

Each year sportswriters and college coaches select the most outstanding players in college football. Those who are chosen are called "All-Americans."

ALL-PRO

Each year professional football coaches and experts in the office of the Pro Football Commissioner select the most outstanding players in pro football. Those chosen are called "All-Pros."

ALL THE WAY

Any play that scores a touchdown. When a

player carries the ball over the goal line, it is said that he went "all the way."

AUDIBLE

Changing the play at the line of scrimmage. Usually, the team in possession of the ball (the offensive team) decides on which play they will use while the players are grouped together in a "huddle." However, when they line up against the opposing team, the quarterback might suddenly see a weak spot in the defense. He might want to change the play that was agreed upon in the huddle. Therefore, while his team is lined up ready to begin the action, the quarterback will yell out the signal for a new play. He will call out a color and a number, such as "Red! Fifty-one!" His teammates know that the color red means he is changing to a new play, and the number, fifty-one, is the new play that will be used. Sometimes the quarterback may *pretend* to call an audible, by using a color that isn't "live." He may call out "Brown! Fifty-three!" His teammates know that they are not using the color brown. Therefore, they will execute the play that was agreed upon in the huddle. Also called "automatic" or "check off."

AUTOMATIC
See Audible.

BACKFIELD (DEFENSIVE)

The team *not* in possession of the ball—the defensive team—uses four men in the backfield: two corner halfbacks and two safety men.

BACKFIELD (OFFENSIVE)

The team in possession of the ball—the offensive team—uses four players in its backfield: a quarterback, a halfback, a fullback, and a flanker back.

BACKFIELD IN MOTION

When the team in possession of the ball lines up to begin a play, no player on that team may move forward until the ball is snapped from the center to the quarterback and the play begins. One of the backfield men is permitted to run *to the side or backward,* but not forward, while the team is lined up. If a backfield man moves even an inch forward before the ball is snapped, an official who sees the man move will stop the play. The team with the ball is penalized five yards for "backfield in motion." Also called "illegal procedure."

BACK JUDGE

One of the officials in a football game is the "back judge." He stands along the "line of scrimmage," and it is his job to see that neither team is "offside," or uses their hands when they are not supposed to. He also assists other officials in their duties. The back judge also helps keep track of the time of the game.

BACKUP MAN

A defensive player who takes up his position a few yards behind a teammate is usually referred to as a "backup man." If his teammate should miss tackling the man with the ball, the backup man might make the tackle.

BACKWARD PASS

See Lateral pass.

BALANCED LINE

When the team in possession of the ball lines up, the forward line (all the players except the backfield) consists of seven players: one center, two guards, two tackles, and two ends. One guard, one tackle, and one end line up on either side of the center, in that order. This is called a "balanced line." A team is also permitted to line up with an "unbalanced line."

SE	OT	OG	C	OG	OT	TE
○	○	○	▣	○	○	○

BALANCED LINE

BALANCED OFFENSE

In order to have a good attack, a team should be able to gain ground equally well either by running with the ball or by passing it. Such a team is said to have a "balanced offense."

BALL CONTROL

A team that can keep possession of the ball by gaining first downs, and not allowing the other team to get the ball, is "controlling the ball." Each time a play is tried, a few yards are gained, and the team keeps on getting first downs until it scores a touchdown.

BASIC T FORMATION

This is one of the oldest kinds of "T formations" in football. Actually, the T formation was used many years ago, but coaches tried out other formations, such as single wing, double wing, and others, so that for many years the T formation was forgotten. Toward the end of the 1930's, the Chicago Bears went back to the old T formation and it proved to be very successful. In this kind of "basic T formation," the quarterback of the offensive team stands right behind the center. The three other backfield men stand about four yards behind the quarterback. Thus the center, the quarterback, and the other backs form themselves into a formation that looks like the letter "T."

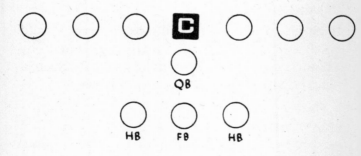

BASIC T FORMATION

BIRD CAGE

The rubber-covered metal tubing that is attached to a player's helmet, to protect his face, is often called a "bird cage" or simply a "face mask."

BIRD CAGE

BLITZ

Sometimes, the defensive linebackers, the corner halfbacks, and even the safety men will suddenly charge toward the line of scrimmage, trying to knock down the quarterback before he has time to drop back for a pass, or before he can hand the ball to another backfield man. Usually, the halfbacks and safety men stay back, to try to stop a forward pass. When the halfbacks and linebackers and safety men dash through the line of scrimmage, they are "blitzing." Also called "red dog."

7

BLOCK

When a team is in possession of the ball, the players on that team are not allowed to use their hands when shoving an opponent out of the way. The ball carrier may use his hand to ward off a tackler, and that is called a "straight arm" or "stiff arm," but he is the only offensive player allowed to use his hands. In order for the other offensive players to push an opponent away, they may use only their body (above the knees) or the arms, provided that the arms are

BLOCK

close to the body. This kind of shoving by an offensive player is called "blocking." *Any* player can use his body or hands to block *the football itself* when it is being kicked or passed.

BLOCKING ASSIGNMENT
Once a play begins, each man on the offensive team must know where to move and which defensive player he will block out of the play. That is his "blocking assignment."

BOMB
A long, high forward pass which is meant to score a touchdown or gain a great many yards.

BOOTLEG
Sometimes a quarterback will pretend to give the ball to his halfback or fullback, but instead he keeps it himself. As the halfback or fullback *fakes* carrying the ball into the line of scrimmage, the quarterback, still holding the ball, tries to hide it alongside his leg, and runs in the opposite direction. If the halfback or fullback is running to the left, the quarterback will run to the right. Also called "keeper."

BOUNDARY LINES
These are the long lines marked out at each side of the field and at each end, defining how long and how wide a football field is.

BOOTLEG

BOXMAN

Standing along the sideline is a man holding a long pole. On top of the pole is a large square frame that looks like a box, with the numbers 1, 2, 3, and 4. These numbers tell what "down" is coming up. The numbers are always turned toward the field, so that the players can see them easily. When it is first down, the number 1 is turned toward the playing field. The man holding the pole to which the number box is attached is called a "boxman."

10

BREAD-AND-BUTTER PLAY

All teams have a favorite offensive play, which they feel sure will gain a few yards, at least most of the time. It is a dependable play.

BRUSH BLOCK

There are times when it is not necessary for an offensive player to block a defensive player for more than an instant. The offensive player merely has to brush his opponent aside, because the man carrying the ball will have run past the defensive player being brush-blocked and will no longer be in danger of getting tackled by him.

BUTTONHOOK

A pass pattern of a receiver as he runs straight

BUTTONHOOK

ahead for a few yards, then stops suddenly and moves back a couple of steps, facing the man who will throw the pass. Also called "comeback pass."

CENTER

An offensive lineman. At the beginning of a play, the center bends over the football, holding it with one or two hands. To start the play's action, he will pass the ball back between his legs to the quarterback, who is crouching right behind him.

CENTER THE BALL

When the center passes the ball back to the quarterback between his legs, that is known as "centering the ball."

CHAIN CREW

Along the sidelines, a group of men are sta-

CENTER THE BALL

tioned, holding the pole with the down numbers (*see* Boxman), and two poles, or rods, connected with a ten-yard piece of chain. When the officials are not quite sure whether or not a first down has been achieved, the chain crew brings the chain onto the field. The referee measures the progress of the ball, to see whether or not it has been advanced at least ten yards from the point where it was a first down. Also called "rod-men."

CHECK OFF
See Audible.

CIRCLE IN
A pass pattern of a receiver as he runs past the line of scrimmage and then curves over toward the center of the field.

CIRCLE OUT
A pass pattern of a receiver as he runs past the line of scrimmage and then curves over toward the sideline nearest him.

CLEATS
The small knobs at the bottom of the players' shoes, which help them dig into the turf of the football field.

CLIP
A block which is *not* legal. An offensive player is not permitted to block a defensive player from behind. A clip is usually a block or shove across the back of a defensive player's legs. When those sharp-eyed officials see that happen, the clipping team will be penalized fifteen yards, and the penalty is marked off from the spot where the clip occurred.

CLIP

COFFIN CORNER
The area near the sideline from the ten-yard line back to the goal line is called the "coffin corner." When an offensive team is forced to give up the ball because it cannot achieve a first down it usually will punt the ball away. The punter hopes that he can kick the ball so that it goes out of bounds between the other team's ten-yard line and its goal line.

COMEBACK PASS
See Buttonhook.

CONVERSION

After the offensive team has scored a touchdown, it has the opportunity to score an additional point (or more) in several different ways. One way is the place-kick. If the kicker can kick the ball so that it passes between the uprights of the goalposts, it counts as one point. If the quarterback throws a pass to a receiver over the goal line, or if a ball carrier can run over the goal line, that is known as a "two-point conversion." The two-point conversion, by running or passing, counts as two points only in college football or in the American Football League. In the National Football League, the conversion by passing or running counts for only one point, the same as the kick.

CORNERBACK

A defensive player, also called a corner halfback, who takes up a position about ten yards from the line of scrimmage, and a few yards from the sideline. Usually, a defensive team has two cornerbacks.

CORNER LINEBACKER

Defensive teams usually use three linebackers, who position themselves a yard or two behind their defensive line, or even at the line of scrimmage. The left linebacker and the right linebacker are called "corner linebackers."

CRACKBACK BLOCK

When a pass receiver runs past the line of scrimmage, then turns and comes back again to block out a defensive player, that maneuver is known as a "crackback block." In 1974, the pro rules were changed to make a crackback block illegal.

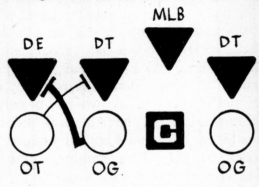

CROSS BLOCK

CROSS BLOCK

Many times an offensive lineman will not try to block the defensive player positioned right in front of him. There are other ways to block an opponent to the side. The diagram shows how this is done.

CROSS PATTERN

Sometimes, two pass receivers will cross paths as they race downfield. This is done to confuse the defensive backfield.

CUP

When the quarterback drops back to pass, several offensive players will move back with him, and form an arc around the passer in order to protect him from the oncoming defensive players. This arc or semicircle is called a "cup" or a "pocket."

CUT

When a running player suddenly changes direction.

DEAD BALL

After a play is completed and the referee blows his whistle, no one may pick up the football except one of the officials. The ball is no longer in play. It is a "dead ball."

DEFENSE

The team *not* in possession of the ball.

DEFENSIVE END

A defensive player stationed at one end of the line of scrimmage. Each defensive team has two defensive ends.

DEFENSIVE TACKLE

A defensive player stationed at the line of scrimmage between the two defensive ends. Each defensive team has two defensive tackles.

DELAY OF GAME

When a play is finished, and the referee or one of the players does not call for a time out, the offensive team has thirty seconds to begin another play. If the new play is not begun in thirty seconds, the referee will impose a five-yard penalty against the offensive team. The offensive team may take more than thirty seconds if the play that was finished was an incompleted pass or if the ball went out of bounds.

DELAYED PASS

After the ball is snapped from the center to the quarterback, a pass receiver might not run out past the line of scrimmage immediately. He may hesitate, as if to block for the quarterback. Then, after that slight "delay," he will run forward to receive the pass.

DIAGRAM

In order for a football coach to show his players what their duties are during each play, he must draw a diagram of the play. It is quite simple to learn a play by following a diagram.

DIVE

A type of running play. The quarterback hands off to a running back, who moves straight ahead to plunge through the line. Generally, this kind of play is used when only one or two yards are needed in order for the offensive team to gain a first down or score a touchdown.

DOUBLE FOUL

If both teams commit a foul during the same play, it is considered a double foul. There is no penalty against either team, and the down does not change.

DOUBLE TEAM

When two defensive players guard one offensive player, such as a linebacker and corner half-back guarding a pass receiver; or when two offensive players guard against one defensive player, such as the center and one guard blocking out the middle linebacker. Any situation that has two players guarding against one player is called "double teaming." Also called "two on one."

DOUBLE WING

An offensive formation. The quarterback stands behind the center. The fullback is about four yards behind the quarterback. The flanker back is near one end of the line of scrimmage, and

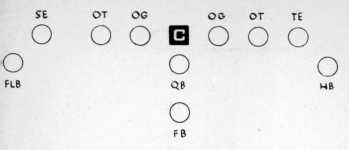

DOUBLE WING

the halfback is near the other end of the line of scrimmage.

DOWN

Each time the offensive team runs with the ball or tries a pass, it is called a *down*. A team is allowed four downs in order to gain at least ten yards.

DOWN-AND-IN

A pass pattern run by a receiver. He runs straight ahead for a few yards, past the line of scrimmage, then turns sharply and runs toward the center of the playing field.

DOWN-AND-OUT

A pass pattern run by a receiver. He runs straight ahead for a few yards, past the line of scrimmage, then turns sharply and runs toward the nearest sideline.

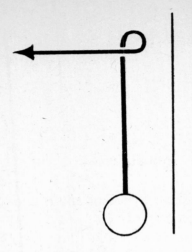

DOWN-AND-IN

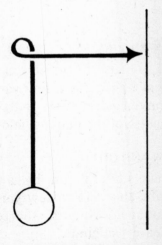

DOWN-AND-OUT

DOWNFIELD

Once an offensive player moves about three yards past the line of scrimmage, he is considered "downfield."

DOWNING THE BALL

On a kickoff that goes beyond the goal line into the end zone, the receiver of the kick may elect not to run with the ball. After catching the ball, he touches the ground with his knee, or by his actions indicates to the officials that he does not intend to run forward with the football. It is an automatic touchback, and the ball is brought out to the twenty-yard line. Also called "grounding the ball."

DRAW PLAY

When the quarterback drops back as if he intends to throw a pass, but suddenly hands the

DRAW PLAY

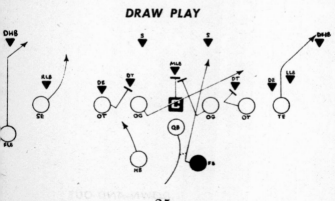

ball to a backfield runner who is pretending to block for him, it is called a "draw play."

DROPKICK

This type of kick is seldom used in modern football. Many years ago, the dropkick was executed when trying for a field goal or point-after-touchdown. Today, the place-kick is used. For a dropkick, the ball is dropped to the ground by the kicker; when it starts to bounce up, the ball is kicked. It is not to be confused with a punt.

EAT THE BALL

On many occasions, a passer can't find a receiver out in the open so that he can throw the ball to him. If the passer throws the ball merely hoping that someone on his team can catch it, the ball may be intercepted by an opposing player. So the passer hugs the ball to his chest and allows the incoming tacklers to knock him down. That is called "eating the ball."

ELIGIBLE RECEIVER

There are only five offensive players permitted to catch a forward pass: the two ends, the halfback, the fullback, and the flanker back. The other offensive players are not eligible (not permitted) to catch a forward pass.

END (DEFENSIVE)

The two players at each end of the line of scrimmage, on the defensive team.

END (OFFENSIVE)

The two players at each end of the line of scrimmage, on the offensive team.

END LINE

The white line at the rear of both end zones.

END SWEEP

A running play around the left or right end of the line of scrimmage.

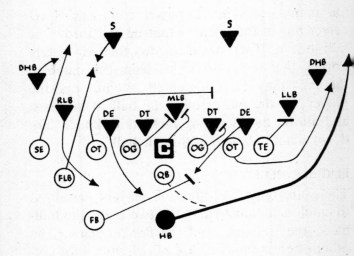

END SWEEP

END ZONE
The touchdown area. It runs the width of the field and is ten yards deep.

EXTRA POINT
The point-after-touchdown. *See* Conversion.

FACE MASK
See Bird cage.

FADE BACK
When the quarterback takes the snap from center and moves back of the line of scrimmage, he is "fading back."

FAIR CATCH
Usually, when the ball is punted, the player receiving the kick will try to run with the ball. But if the receiver sees the opposing players are so close that he will be tackled immediately, and possibly fumble the ball, he may signal for a "fair catch." He raises one arm over his head,

which means that he will only catch the ball, but not try to run back with it. No opponent is permitted to touch him while he catches the ball. If they do, it means a fifteen-yard penalty. If the receiver fumbles the ball, the opposing players are permitted to go after it; it is a free ball.

FAKE

Any motion meant to deceive or fool players on the other team is called a "fake." It can be a fake hand-off, a fake run, a fake pass, or a fake move in one direction, followed by a real move in the opposite direction.

FIELD GOAL

To place-kick the ball between the goalposts (*not* after a touchdown). A field goal counts for three points.

FIELD-GOAL RANGE

Most good pro field-goal kickers can usually kick the ball through the uprights (the goalposts) from as far as fifty yards away. When an offensive team reaches its opponents' thirty-yard line, a pro kicker can often make the field goal easily. The ball is said to be in "field-goal range" when it reaches about the thirty-yard line of the other team.

FIELD JUDGE

One of the officials at a game. His duties include timing the intermission between periods and between each half, the length of each time out, the time allowed the offensive team to put the ball into play again (each team is permitted thirty seconds after the finish of one play to start another play, except for incomplete passes or plays that end out of bounds), and to cover the action on kicks and passes downfield.

FILL THE GAP

When an offensive lineman moves out of the line of scrimmage in order to lead the interference on a running play, a teammate has to fill the hole or "gap" the lineman has left.

FIRST DOWN

The offensive team, when it first gets the ball, has four chances to gain at least ten yards. When it gains ten yards, it achieves a first down, and then has four more chances to achieve another first down.

FLAG

At the four corners of the "0 yard line" (the goal line) at each end of the field there are small flags planted in the ground. A pass receiver, running toward one of the flags, is said to be "running a flag pattern."

FLAG ON THE PLAY

Officials carry pieces of colored cloth, somewhat like big colored handkerchiefs. When an official sees an infraction of the rules, he throws the cloth on the ground at the spot where the infraction was committed. That means the play is called back, there is a "flag on the play," and a penalty will be marked off against one of the teams. Also called "penalty marker."

FLANK

The area between the end (or flanker back) and the sideline. Also called "flat."

FLANKER BACK

One of the four offensive backfield men.

FLARE PASS

A pass thrown to a backfield man generally behind the line of scrimmage. Also called "flat pass."

FLAT (ZONE)

See Flank.

FLOOD

In order to confuse defensive halfbacks and safety men, the offensive team will send two, three, or four potential pass receivers to the same side of the field (right side or left side). Thus there are more possible receivers than defensive players in that area.

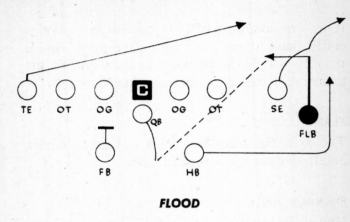

FLOOD

FLOW OF PLAY
The direction in which the play moves.

FLY
A pass pattern run by a receiver. He does not cut in any direction; instead, he races ahead as fast as he can, hoping to outrun the defensive player guarding him, get behind the defensive player, receive the pass, and run for a long gain or touchdown. Usually, only the fastest receivers, such as Homer Jones of the Giants or Bob Hayes of the Dallas Cowboys, will specialize in running the fly pattern.

FLY

FORWARD MOTION

The movement of a ball carrier toward the defensive team's goal line.

FORWARD PASS

Any pass that is thrown by an offensive player in the direction of the defensive team's goal line is a forward pass. It doesn't matter if the pass is caught behind the line of scrimmage or beyond the line of scrimmage. If the ball is thrown forward, it is considered a forward pass.

FOUL

Any time the rules of football are broken, a foul has been committed.

FREE BALL

A ball in possession of neither team is called a free ball. After a fumble or a dropped kickoff or punt reception, the first player to fall on the ball or grab and hold it gains possession for his team.

FREE KICK

There are certain situations when a kicker may punt the ball, or place-kick the ball, and the opposing team is not permitted to interfere with the kicker. No one may try to block the kick. These situations include: after a touchdown or field goal has been scored, the scoring team kicks off to the opposing team by place-kicking the ball; after a safety has been scored, the team that has been *scored against* must punt (or place-kick) the ball to the scoring team, from its own twenty-yard line; when a player signals for a fair catch, his team may, if it desires, place-kick the ball in an attempt to score a field goal. The latter situation is rare, but it is part of the rules of football.

FREE SAFETY

Usually, there are two safety men on a defensive team. One of them will not have the responsibility of guarding against a specific receiver. He is permitted to move wherever he thinks the play will come. Most of the time he is stationed on the "weak side" in relation to the offensive team.

FRONT FOUR

On the defensive team, the two ends and two tackles are referred to as the "front four."

FULLBACK

One of the four offensive backfield men. As a rule the fullback is the strongest and heaviest of the ball carriers. Most of the time he is called upon to carry the ball into the line, to pick up two or three yards for a first down, although he has other duties as well.

FUMBLE

When a player in possession of the ball drops it, either by being tackled hard, or allowing the ball to slip out of his hands, or by any other means, he has "fumbled" the ball.

FUNDAMENTALS

The basic skills of football (or any other sport). The fundamentals of football include blocking, tackling, catching the ball, passing the ball, running with the ball, defending against passes and against running plays.

GANG TACKLE
Two or more defensive players combining to tackle the ball carrier.

GAP
The space between two offensive or defensive linemen.

GOAL LINE
The final chalk line before the end zone is reached.

GOALPOSTS
The "H" formed by two vertical bars and the horizontal crossbar. Some professional goalposts are shaped like a "Y."

GRIDIRON

A football field is sometimes referred to as a "gridiron."

GROUNDING THE BALL

When a passer finds no receivers in the clear, he will sometimes throw the ball in such a way that if his own receiver cannot reach it, neither can an opposing defensive player intercept it. Also called "intentional grounding."

HALF

The middle point of a football game. All football games are divided into four quarters. There is a one-minute rest between the first and second period, and between the third and fourth period. Between the second and third period, there is a rest of fifteen minutes or more. It is between the halves of a game that the school bands put on their "halftime shows."

HALFBACK (DEFENSIVE)

See Cornerback.

HALFBACK (OFFENSIVE)

An offensive backfield player. Usually, he is

lighter and faster than his fullback teammate, but many of the duties are equally shared by both of these backfield players. One or the other will carry the football on running plays.

HAND-OFF

For running plays, the quarterback will "hand the ball" to either the halfback or fullback (and sometimes, on special plays, to the flanker back or end).

HASHMARKS

Between the five-yard-line markers are smaller marks which are spaced one yard apart. These are called "hashmarks." *See also* Inbound lines.

HELMET

The protective headgear worn by all football players.

HIGH-LOW

When a player is blocked (or tackled) by two opposing players, sometimes one blocker (or tackler) will hit the opposing player "high," around the chest or shoulders, while his teammate hits him "low," around the legs or below the knees.

HUDDLE

In order to discuss the strategy of a play, offensive players often gather in a small circle behind the line of scrimmage. Sometimes they do not form a circle, but stand in two rows, one behind the other, facing the quarterback, while he explains which play he will call. Defensive players also discuss their strategy in a huddle.

I FORMATION

An offensive formation, with three backfield players lined up one behind the other.

```
 ◯     ◯  ◯  🄲  ◯  ◯  ◯
SE     OT OG    OG OT TE
              ◯              ◯
              QB             FL
            ◯ HB.
            ◯ FB
```

I FORMATION

ILLEGAL MOTION
See In motion.

INBOUND LINES

These are "hashmarks" or lines that are drawn parallel to the sidelines. When the ball goes out of bounds, it is brought back into the playing field and placed down on one of these hashmarks. In college football, the hashmarks are fifty-three feet, four inches from the sidelines. In professional football, they are seventy feet, nine inches from the sidelines.

INELIGIBLE RECEIVER

Only five offensive players are permitted to receive a forward pass from the quarterback: the three players in the backfield and the two players at the end of the line of scrimmage. All others are "ineligible"—not permitted to catch a forward pass.

IN MOTION

Before the start of a play, while the quarterback is calling the signals, one of the other backfield players (usually the fullback or halfback) is permitted to run parallel to, or slightly backward from, the line of scrimmage. All other offensive players cannot move once they are in set position.

INTERCEPTION

A defensive player catching any kind of pass (forward or lateral) which is intended for an offensive player.

INTERFERENCE

There are two kinds of interference. (1) One type has an offensive player running ahead of the ball carrier to block out defensive players. The blocker is said to be "running interference." (2) In this case, interference refers to illegally hindering another player. Most often it happens during a pass play. When an offensive receiver is trying to catch a forward pass, and a defensive player pushes him or gets in his way *before* he makes the catch, the defensive player is guilty of interference. The same rule applies to a player who is attempting to catch a punt and is interfered with by a player from the opposing team.

INTERIOR LINEMAN

Generally refers to the offensive guards, tackles, and center.

J

JUKING

Often, in order to confuse the offensive players, the four defensive linemen and the defensive linebackers will begin changing positions. For example, one linebacker may suddenly move right up into the line of scrimmage alongside his teammate, then suddenly jump right back to his original position before the ball is snapped. Also called "stunting."

JUMP PASS

This type of pass is not often executed. The quarterback leaps high and throws a forward pass while still in the air. In the past, quarterbacks sometimes leaped high in order to see over the huge linemen who were rushing in at them.

KEEPER

See Bootleg.

KEY

Key, or "keying in on," refers to how offensive and defensive players react. For example, when a team has an outstanding pass receiver, there will always be one and sometimes two defensive players guarding him no matter where he goes or what he does. Even if the pass receiver is merely faking, or being used as a decoy while some other receiver catches the pass, the star receiver will always be followed by the defensive players assigned to guard or to "key in on" him. When the great Jimmy Brown was playing for the Cleveland Browns, there were always one or two defensive players assigned to key in on him no matter what kind of play was being used, whether he carried the ball or not.

KICKER

The offensive player who is a specialist at punting or place-kicking. Some teams have one man who is a good punter and another who is a good place-kicker, so that there are two kickers on the club.

KICKING TEE

For kickoffs and place-kicking for a conversion or field goal, a small device to hold the ball steady is used. For kickoffs, the ball is propped up on the kicking tee and no one is needed to hold the ball at its point. For place-kicking for a conversion, one offensive player kneels, takes the snap from the center, and places the ball on the kicking tee for the kicker.

KICKING UNIT

In pro football, there are special teams which are used in kicking situations (for example, when it is fourth down and many yards to go for a first down, so that the offensive team is sure to kick the ball away). These men are seldom first-string regulars, but are mostly substitutes. *See also* Suicide squad.

KICKOFF

After every touchdown or field goal, or at the start of each half, the ball is place-kicked from the kicking team's thirty-five yard line.

LATERAL PASS

A pass thrown *to the side or backward*. It can be used behind the line of scrimmage, or when a ball carrier has passed the line of scrimmage and wishes to pass the ball to a teammate. Also called "backward pass."

LEAD

When a pass receiver is racing downfield, a good passer will try to throw the ball in such a way that the receiver will catch up with the football. The passer throws the ball ahead of the receiver —that is, he "leads" him.

51

LINEBACKER

Defensive teams have three linebackers, who are usually stationed about two or three yards behind the defensive line. Sometimes the linebackers will move up so that they themselves are practically in the defensive line, especially when they feel sure that the offensive team will try a run through the line.

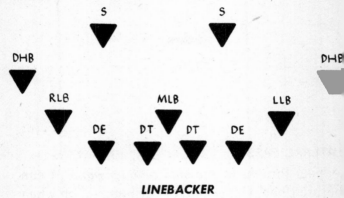

LINEBACKER

LINEMAN

One of the players, offensive or defensive, stationed at the line of scrimmage.

LINE OF SCRIMMAGE

This is really an imaginary line. If there were such a line, it would be where the football is placed at the end of each play. The two teams line up on either side of the imaginary line, facing each other.

LINESMAN

The official who is responsible for all the actions that take place at the line of scrimmage (such as offside). The head linesman also takes charge of the chain crew. He tries to follow all the action that takes place on his side of the field.

LOFT A PASS

To throw a high forward pass a long way downfield.

LONG MAN

The pass receiver who moves farthest downfield.

LOOK-IN PASS

Instead of dropping back, the quarterback takes the snap from center, straightens up, and throws the ball almost immediately to an end or flanker who slants toward the middle of the field, right behind the defensive line.

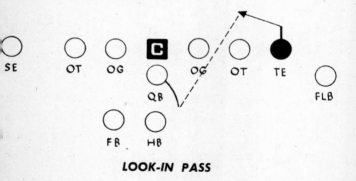

LOOK-IN PASS

LOOPING

Most of the time, a defensive lineman or linebacker will charge straight ahead, trying to
break up a play or get to the quarterback before
the latter has a chance to pass. But sometimes,
the defensive players up front will switch positions, in order to confuse the offensive blockers.
The left end may move straight ahead, while the
left tackle might move through the spot left
open by his left-end teammate. It is almost the
same as juking, but "looping" takes place *after*
a play has started, while juking is done before
the play gets under way.

LOOSE BALL

When a fumble occurs and anyone can grab the
ball.

MAN-FOR-MAN
When each defensive player is assigned one offensive player. Most often, man-for-man refers to the assignments of the defensive secondary, each of whom is responsible for guarding a particular pass receiver.

MAN-IN-MOTION
See In motion.

MEASURING CHAIN
See Yard chain.

MIDFIELD
The fifty-yard line.

MULTIPLE FOUL

Two or more fouls committed by one team on the same play.

NEUTRAL ZONE

Almost the same as the line of scrimmage. This is the area between the offensive and defensive lines as they line up facing each other. The neutral zone is about as wide as the length of a football.

NUMBERING SYSTEM

The next time you watch a football game, notice the numbers on the backs of the players' jerseys. The numbering system is not really official, and there are no written rules to follow, but nearly all teams use the system because it is traditional:

The numbers from 1 to 19 are for the quarterbacks. From 20 to 29 and from 40 to 49 are reserved for the halfbacks. Numbers from 30 to 39 are given to the fullbacks. From 50 to 59 are for centers and linebackers. From 60 to 69 are for guards. From 70 to 79 are for the tackles. Numbers from 80 to 89 are given to ends and flankers.

OFFENSE

The team in possession of the ball.

OFFICIALS' SIGNALS

Football officials use a set of hand and arm signals to inform players, coaches, and spectators of the progress of the game. Each signal has a special meaning. For example, should the referee place both hands on his hips and point to one of the teams, that would signify the team was offside. Raising both arms aloft would signify that a score has been made—a touchdown, a field goal, or a conversion. See pages 60-65 for all officials' signals.

CLIPPING

DEAD BALL

FIRST DOWN

GAME DELAY

ILLEGAL FORWARD PASS

HOLDING

ILLEGAL MOTION

INTERFERENCE

LOSS OF DOWN

OFFSIDE

NO TIME OUT

PENALTY REFUSED

PERSONAL FOUL

TIME OUT

SAFETY

PUSHING

TOUCHDOWN

UNSPORTSMANLIKE CONDUCT

OFFSIDE

Before the ball is snapped, no player from either team may cross the line of scrimmage. If a player does move across the scrimmage line and makes contact with an opposing player, then the player who moved is considered offside, and his team is penalized five yards.

OFF-TACKLE PLAY

A drive into the line by a ball carrier who tries to move through a hole between the offensive tackle and the offensive guard.

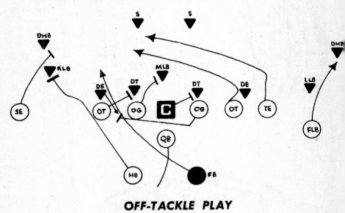

OFF-TACKLE PLAY

OFF THE BALL

This expression is football slang, and refers to how fast a lineman can move after the ball has been snapped from center to the quarterback. If the lineman moves quickly, just a fraction of a second after the snap, he is "off the ball early." Such a lineman has good reflexes and is valuable to his team.

ONSIDE KICK

A kickoff, which takes place after a touch-down or field goal has been scored, or at the start of each half, can be recovered by the kicking team if it is lucky. The kicker will not kick the ball hard; he will simply tap it, sometimes with the side of his foot. He does not want the ball to travel far, but just far enough to reach the opposing team's forty-yard line. If a player on the kicking team is fortunate enough to reach the ball before anyone on the receiving team, then the kicking team takes possession of the ball.

OPTION PLAY

For the most part, college football players use the option play. The pros use it sometimes, but in a different way. And the pros only try the option play when a halfback or fullback is a good passer as well as runner. This is how it works:

In college football, the quarterback takes the snap from center and runs behind the line of scrimmage. His halfback or fullback is a couple of yards to the side. If the quarterback thinks he can gain several yards by running, he keeps the ball. If he is in danger of being tackled before he can gain a few yards, he throws a lateral pass to the nearby halfback or fullback, who continues to run with the ball.

In pro football, the quarterback will hand off to his halfback or fullback, who runs toward the sidelines, as if to execute an end sweep. If he thinks he can gain ground, he will keep the ball and continue to run around end with it. But if he sees a defensive halfback or linebacker move up to tackle him, then the ball carrier will throw a pass to a receiver, who has moved into the area left open by the defensive halfback or linebacker. One of the best halfback-passers in pro football is Gale Sayers of the Chicago Bears. On several occasions he has thrown passes that scored touchdowns.

OUT IN THE OPEN
When a pass receiver fools a defensive player assigned to guard him, so that neither he nor any other defensive player is near him, the receiver is said to be "out in the open."

OUT OF BOUNDS
Beyond the sidelines. When the ball or the ball carrier goes out of bounds, the clock is stopped, and does not start again until the beginning of the following play.

OVERSHIFT

If the offensive team lines up in such a way that the running backs and two pass receivers are all stationed on one side, the defensive team will shift its players to that same side. They will line up so that more defensive players are ready to take care of the receivers and runners on that side of the line. The defense is then "overshifted."

PASS
Throwing the ball from one player to another.

PASS PATTERN
The way a pass receiver runs when he moves away from the line of scrimmage. He may run straight ahead, then cut sharply to the sidelines, or come back toward the receiver a few steps, or slant to either side.

PASSING SITUATION
When it is second or third down, and the offensive team must still gain considerable yardage in order to achieve a first down, the best way

to gain ground quickly is by a forward pass. Therefore, it is called a "passing situation."

PENALTY

The yardage lost by a team for breaking the rules of football.

PENALTY MARKER

See Flag on the play.

PERIOD

A football game is divided into four 15-minute quarters. Each quarter is called "a period."

PERSONAL FOUL

There are really two kinds of football penalties. One has to do with violation of the basic rules of the game, such as offside, illegal motion, ineligible player downfield. The other type pertains to breaking of the rules by one or more players in a *violent* way, such as unnecessary roughness, punching another player, kicking him, clipping, players needlessly piling on a tackled ball carrier, roughing the passer or roughing the kicker, shoving or otherwise interfering with a pass receiver. The second type is a *personal* foul. It was committed by one person against another, not merely breaking the rules of the game but being guilty of poor sportsmanship.

PILE ON

After a ball carrier (or any other player) is down on the ground and the whistle blows, no one else may tackle or fall on the downed player. Breaking this rule means a penalty of fifteen yards. Sometimes, after a tackle has been made, another opponent will be moving toward the downed man so fast that he can't stop himself in time, and he accidentally falls on the downed man. It is up to the officials to decide if such an action was deliberate or accidental. If it was an accident and the defensive player could not possibly stop himself in time, there is no penalty.

PITCHOUT

A short pass thrown by the quarterback to a halfback or fullback who is out in the flat zone.

PLACE-KICK

To kick the ball while it is being held point-down on the ground by a teammate, or when the ball is placed point-down on a kicking tee. Sometimes, as when a team is going to attempt an onside kick, the ball will be placed down flat.

PLAY ACTION PASS

Instead of dropping back to throw a forward pass, the quarterback first executes a fake hand-off to his halfback or fullback. There is some

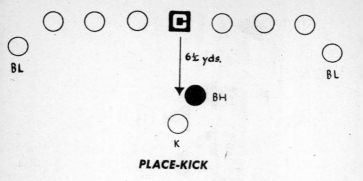

6½ yds.

BH

K

BL

BL

PLACE-KICK

action first, as if for a running play. Instead of having the offensive linemen drop back to protect the passer, this play has them charging straight ahead, as if the play were really going to be a running play; then the quarterback passes.

PLAY BOOK

All players, whether on the offensive or defensive unit of a team, must know what their assignments are for any play. Once they make the team, the players are each given a "play book," which contains diagrams of various offensive and defensive formations, with each man's assignment clearly shown.

POCKET
See Cup.

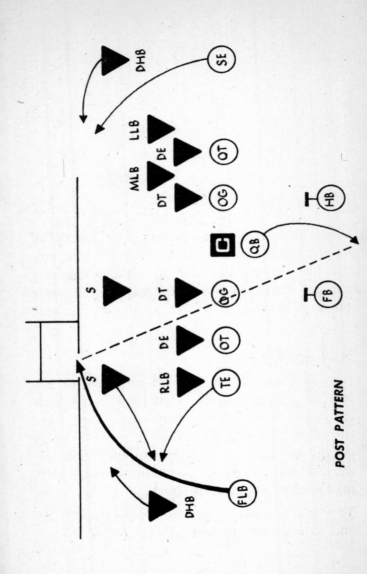

POST PATTERN

POINT-AFTER-TOUCHDOWN

See Conversion.

POST PATTERN

A pass pattern run by a receiver. For this type of play, the receiver races along the sideline, then cuts across the field on a slant, toward the goalposts.

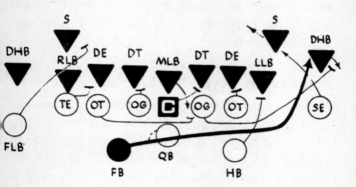

POWER SWEEP

POWER SWEEP

Same as end sweep, except that in the power sweep there are at least two linemen blocking for the ball carrier. Also, he moves in a kind of arc first before moving around end.

PREVENT DEFENSE

This is a defensive formation used by halfbacks and safety men against passes. When the defensive team has a lead of six or seven points, late in the game, they know that the offensive team will throw passes in order to try to score a touchdown. It is always possible that a long forward pass will succeed, and either gain a great many yards or even score the touchdown. Therefore, the defensive backs will play "deep." This kind of defensive formation allows the offensive team to complete only the short passes, which do not gain much ground. It *prevents* the long pass from being completed.

PRIMARY RECEIVER

When a pass play is agreed upon in the huddle, usually the play calls for the quarterback to throw the ball to a particular receiver. It may be the end or one of the backs. The one for whom the pass is intended is the primary receiver. If that man is too well guarded, the quarterback may throw the ball to another receiver, a "safety valve."

PULL OUT OF THE LINE

On certain running plays, such as end sweeps, the offensive guards are required to run interference. They do not charge straight ahead, but step back from the line ("pull out of the line"), run behind the line of scrimmage, then lead the interference around end.

PUNT

When a team has tried three plays and realizes that it cannot achieve a first down on the next play, it will kick the ball to the opposing team. This type of kick is called a punt. The kicker will stand about fifteen yards behind the line of scrimmage, take the snap from center and kick the ball. A punt is different from a place-kick or dropkick in that the ball does not touch the ground before it is kicked away.

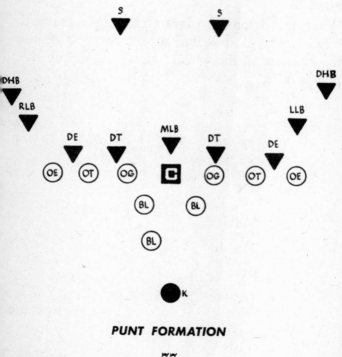

PUNT FORMATION

PUNT FORMATION

When the offensive team finds that it cannot achieve a first down in four plays, it will usually punt the ball away on fourth down. The team lines up in a special formation called "punt formation."

PUNT RETURN

Running back upfield with the ball after receiving the punt.

PURSUIT

When the defensive players race after the ball carrier with all possible speed, never stopping the chase until the whistle blows, signifying the play is over.

Q

QUARTER

See Period.

QUARTERBACK

One of the offensive backfield players. He is the "field general," calling the plays in the huddle. The quarterback is almost always the passer, except when he hands off the ball on an option play.

QUARTERBACK DRAW

The quarterback drops back as if to pass, then tucks the ball under his arm and runs with it. Most of the time he runs straight ahead if there is a hole in the middle of the line. But he might also run on a slant, toward any opening he sees.

QUARTERBACK SNEAK

Same as bootleg or keeper, except that this type of play is used when only a yard or two is needed for a first down or touchdown.

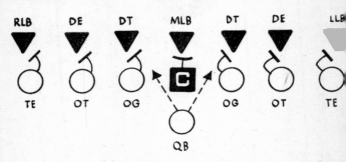

QUARTERBACK SNEAK

QUICK OPENER

A running play. The quarterback hands off quickly to the halfback or fullback, who dives straight ahead through an opening in the line. There is no fake or other deception on this type of play.

QUICK RELEASE

This football term has two different meanings. (1) The first pertains to blocking. An offensive lineman will block out a defensive player for only a moment, hardly longer than a brush

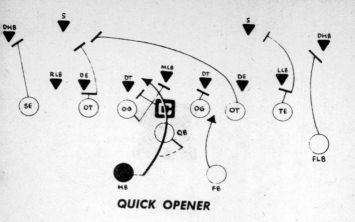

QUICK OPENER

block. Then he moves forward to block out another defensive player. (2) The second meaning refers to the way a quarterback throws a pass. Some passers take a second or two longer than others to "get rid of the ball"; it takes them longer to release the ball. When a passer throws quickly after he cocks his arm, he is said to have a "quick release."

READ THE DEFENSE

Quite often an experienced quarterback can glance at the defense, while he is calling the signals, and, just by observing where the defensive players are stationed, he can find a weak spot, or "read the defense." That is the time he calls an "automatic," changing the play, so he can take advantage of the weakness he has seen.

READ THE OFFENSE

Smart defensive players can figure out what the offense will do, just by observing the offensive players. Sometimes an offensive player will unwittingly "tip off" the type of play that is coming up. One college player often gave away the kind of play the offense was about to use: If he was going to run to the right, he would take his stance leaning to the right. If he was going to carry the ball around to his left, he would lean to his left. It took time before his coach found out what he was doing wrong. After the mistake in the player's stance was corrected, the defense could no longer "read" the type of play coming up.

RECEIVER

A player who receives a pass. Only five offensive players are eligible to receive a forward pass from the quarterback: the two ends, the flanker back, halfback, and fullback. Also called a receiver is the player who catches either a kick-off or a punt.

RED DOG

See Blitz.

REFEREE

The top official in a football game. He paces off the penalties, blows the whistle to signal a dead ball, and places the ball down at the spot where it will be put in play. He is stationed behind the offensive backfield at the start of each play.

REVERSE

A running play that starts out in one direction

and then moves to the other side. There are
several ways to execute the reverse plays. The
quarterback may take the ball from center,
move a couple of steps to his right, and then
hand the ball to a backfield man or end, who
is running in the opposite direction. If the
quarterback hands the ball to one backfield
man, who then, in turn, hands it to another
offensive backfield man, that would be a "double reverse." A "triple reverse" is also used
sometimes.

RODMEN
See Chain crew.

ROLLOUT
When the quarterback runs toward the sidelines, behind the line of scrimmage, before
throwing the ball, the maneuver is called a
"rollout."

ROUGHING THE KICKER OR PASSER
Once a kicker has punted the ball away or tried
a place-kick, or once a passer has thrown a
pass, no opposing player can touch him. Should
the kicker or passer be hit after the kick or
pass has been attempted, it is a foul, and the
penalty is an automatic first down for the fouled
team, plus fifteen yards from the line of scrimmage.

RUNBACK

The return of a punt, an intercepted pass, or a kickoff.

RUNNING BACK

The offensive halfback and fullback are referred to as the running backs.

RUSHING

The yards gained by running with the ball. This pertains to offensive running backs only.

S

SAFETY

When an offensive player, in possession of the ball, is tackled *behind his own goal line,* it counts as two points for the defensive team. The offensive team must then kick the ball to the opposing team, from its own twenty-yard line.

SAFETY BLITZ

Normally, the safety man is positioned about ten or fifteen yards behind his own line. Sometimes, as a surprise maneuver, he will begin to dash toward the line of scrimmage just before the ball is snapped from center to quarterback. The safety man will try to rush in, or "blitz," in order to tackle the quarterback or other back-field man who has the ball.

SAFETY MAN

There are two safety men on a defensive team. They are stationed from ten to fifteen yards behind the line of scrimmage. As a rule, they are assigned to defend against passes. When the offensive team is faced with a "kicking situation" (fourth down and many yards to go before a first down can be achieved), sometimes two safety men will drop back to receive the kicked ball; however, many times only one safety man will be back awaiting the kick.

SAFETY VALVE

Any offensive backfield player or end is permitted to receive a forward pass. Most of the time, when the quarterback calls for a forward pass in the huddle—one intended for a flanker or end—one or both of the running backs will stay near the quarterback in order to block for him. If the flanker or end for whom the pass is intended is too well guarded, and the quarterback sees the defensive team charging in, he may try to pass the ball to one of the running backs, who may not be guarded at the moment. Such a pass is a "safety valve" pass; the receiver is the "safety valve."

SCRAMBLE

In pro football, the quarterback most often tries to throw a forward pass from the protection of the "cup" or "pocket." However, sometimes the defensive players may slip through the blockers, or knock them down. The quarterback no longer has any protection. So he will run about, behind the line of scrimmage, desperately trying to find a receiver who is not guarded, so that he can throw a forward pass to him. The act of running around in that particular situation is called "scrambling."

SCREEN PASS

This is a tricky kind of pass, and it requires a great deal of faking on the part of the offensive team.

A successful screen pass depends on perfect timing! The quarterback takes the snap from center and drops back as if to throw a regular pass. The split end and flanker back race out and execute their pass cuts in normal fashion. The offensive left guard, the fullback and halfback pretend to form a pocket for the passer's protection.

But all these moves are really only fakes to confuse the opposing team. The center and offensive right guard block the middle linebacker and defensive tackle *only momentarily,* then move over to the right side of the playing field.

The offensive left guard, who had pretended to form part of the pass pocket, also moves to the right side of the field. The offensive right tackle does not even pretend to block, but also moves to the right. The tight end executes a square-out pattern to the right so that he too is in position on the right side.

As the defensive team comes in, the quarterback drops back even farther than before. As he does so, the halfback stops faking his blocking assignment and moves to the right. Now there are at least three blockers (and possibly four if the tight end is in the right position) to the right side of the field.

The halfback runs over behind these blockers. The quarterback throws an easy forward

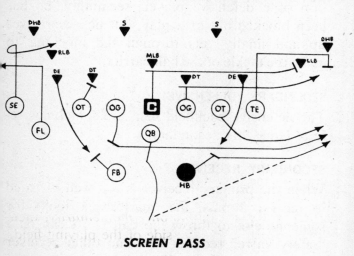

SCREEN PASS

pass over the heads of the incoming defensive players. The halfback catches the pass and moves downfield behind his blockers.

If the timing is perfect, most of the defensive linemen and linebackers will be behind the halfback. His blockers will take care of the rest of the defensive team. Many a touchdown has been scored on a well-timed screen pass!

SECOND EFFORT

A ball carrier's strength and determination are what make the "second effort" possible. When it appears that he has been stopped by the defense, suddenly, with a new display of power, the ball carrier drives forward even farther. A "second effort" also shows the great determination of a defensive player; seemingly, he has been blocked out of a play, but he never gives up and finally gets through the blocking to make the tackle of the ball carrier.

SECONDARY (DEFENSIVE)

The defensive backfield men are sometimes referred to as "the secondary."

SECONDARY RECEIVER

When the primary receiver is too well guarded to receive a pass, the quarterback looks for someone else to throw the ball to. It can be a "safety valve" receiver or some other receiver who has run downfield in order to be ready for just such an emergency.

SERIES OF DOWNS
The four plays in succession which are permitted an offensive team to try for a first down.

SET BACK
An offensive running back, who is positioned about four yards directly behind the quarterback. The other running back and the flanker back are behind and to one side of the quarterback.

SHOESTRING CATCH
Catching a low pass (or punt) when it is near the ground, almost at shoetop level.

SHOESTRING TACKLE
Tackling a ball carrier between the knees and ankles.

SHOOT THE GAP
When offensive blockers pull out of the line in order to block for the quarterback or a ball carrier, or when the defensive line has succeeded in knocking down or "clearing away" some of the offensive blockers, there is a "hole" or "gap" in the line of scrimmage. The defensive

linebackers or some other defensive backfield players go charging through the gap left open.

SHOTGUN

This is almost always a passing formation, and is not used too often, for it is difficult to mount a running attack from the shotgun formation. The quarterback stands about five yards behind his center. The running backs and the flanker back are spread out near the line of scrimmage. In the shotgun formation, the quarterback does not have to spend time dropping back to pass, for he is already back almost far enough, so that he only has to take a step or two to the rear in order to be back far enough to pass.

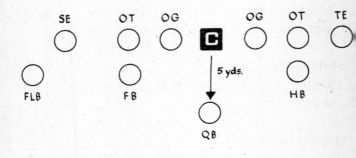

SHOTGUN

SIDELINE PASS

A pass play that has the receiver racing along the sidelines.

92

SINGLE WING

An offensive formation that is no longer widely used. The fullback (called a tailback in this formation) lines up about five yards behind the middle of the offensive line. The other running back is about a yard or two away from him, also about five yards behind the scrimmage line. The quarterback is about a yard behind the line of scrimmage, between the center and the end. The fourth back (called the wingback) is about a yard behind the line, outside his end.

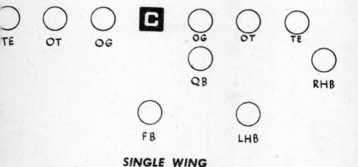

SINGLE WING

SLANT

This can be either a running play or a pass play. When the slant is a running play, the ball carrier takes the hand-off and moves diagonally into the line of scrimmage. On a pass play, the receiver races ahead a couple of yards, then moves diagonally behind the defensive linebackers.

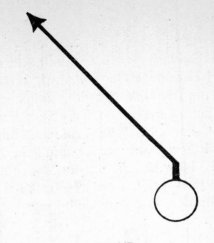

SLANT

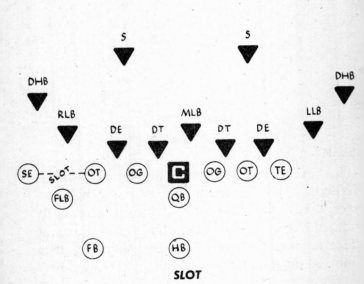

SLOT

SLOT

The opening in the offensive line between the tackle and the split end. When the flanker or a running back stands just behind that gap in the offensive line, he is called a "slot back."

SNAP FROM CENTER

When the center moves the ball between his legs. Should he be giving it to the quarterback, who is right behind him, then the center is practically handing the ball to him. For punts or place-kicks, the center must pass the ball back through his legs.

SPECIAL TEAM

See Kicking unit; Suicide squad.

SPLIT END

One of the offensive ends, who lines up at the

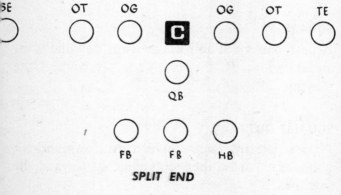

SPLIT END

scrimmage line, about six or seven yards away from his offensive tackle teammate.

SPLIT T

A type of T formation, with the split end stationed wide on one side, and the flanker back wide on the other side.

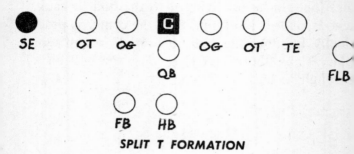

SPLIT T FORMATION

SPREAD END

See Split end.

SQUARE IN

A pass pattern. The receiver runs downfield for about ten yards, then cuts sharply toward the playing field.

SQUARE OUT

A pass pattern. The receiver runs downfield for about ten yards, then cuts sharply toward the sidelines.

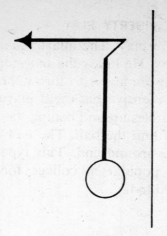

SQUARE IN

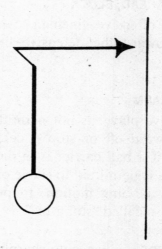

SQUARE OUT

STATUE OF LIBERTY PLAY

An offensive play. The quarterback drops back as if to pass. He holds the ball near his ear, as though he were about to throw the ball. Meanwhile, an offensive backfield player, or one of the ends, circles around behind the quarterback, who hands him the ball. The ball carrier keeps on running around end. This type of play was once very popular in college football, but is seldom used today.

STIFF ARM

See Straight arm.

STRAIGHT-AHEAD BLOCK

When an offensive lineman charges straight forward toward the defensive lineman facing him.

STRAIGHT ARM

An offensive player is not permitted to use his hands to ward off or stop a defensive player. However, if a ball carrier is in danger of being tackled, he is permitted to shove out his hand in a straight, jabbing motion, to push away the tackler. Also called "stiff arm."

STRONG SIDE

In a T formation lineup, the side where the

flanker back and tight end are positioned is called the strong side.

STUNTING
See Juking.

SUBMARINE
When a player moves ahead and keeps his body close to the ground, he is "submarining." A tackle made by a player who has been crouched down is often called "a submarine tackle."

SUBSTITUTE
A player who is not a regular starter. Substitutes get into the game in order to rest the regulars.

SUDDEN-DEATH OVERTIME
In championship games, there can be no tie score. One team or the other must win. Should the score be tied at the end of regulation time (four 15-minute periods) then the game must continue. The referee tosses a coin to see which team kicks off or receives. Then, the first team to score, through a safety, field goal, or touchdown, is declared the winner. One championship game in the American Football League, in 1962, went into the *sixth* period before the Dallas Texans (now the Kansas City Chiefs) defeated the Houston Oilers by a score of 20–17.

SUICIDE SQUAD

The special team of players used on kickoffs. Most of the members of the suicide squad are rookies or substitutes, trying to impress the coach that they are good enough to be playing on the regular defensive or offensive team. They race downfield under the ball, throwing caution to the winds, trying to make hard tackles. These players take chances, and so have earned the nickname "members of the suicide squad."

SWEEP

See End sweep.

SWING PASS

See Flare pass.

TACKLE

The word "tackle" can refer to a position on the team, or it can refer to the way a defensive man stops the ball carrier, by grabbing him and throwing him to the ground. Tackles are executed by grabbing the ball carrier around the legs, jumping on his back or seizing him around the chest, or even the neck.

TAILBACK

The offensive fullback in a single wing formation. He is stationed about five yards behind the center.

TAXI SQUAD

Some pro football players are not quite good enough, or experienced enough, to be on the team. Yet they may develop into good players later on, with more practice. Such players are not released from the team. They are given contracts. These men can practice with the team, but are not on the team's roster of players, which means they cannot get into a real game. However, if one of the players is injured, then a man from the "taxi squad" can be placed on the team.

T FORMATION

There are several different kinds of T formations. Basically, the quarterback lines up directly behind the center; the fullback, halfback, and flanker back line up a few yards behind the quarterback, so that the center, quarterback, and all the backfield men form a letter "T." There are several variations, including split T, slot T, double wing T, and others.

THREE-POINT STANCE

The basic stance assumed by a football player, his feet spread apart, and crouched down with one hand touching the ground in front of him.

TIGHT END

An offensive player positioned near the tackle

THREE-POINT STANCE

at the end of the line. He is usually assigned to block on some running plays and to catch passes. *Compare with* Split end.

TIGHT SAFETY

The defensive safety man who will guard the tight end on pass plays.

TIME IN

The clock is running, the game is progressing. That is time in.

TIME OUT

There are several reasons for stopping the play of a game, including the times when the ball goes out of bounds, for a fair catch, when a foul has been committed, after an incomplete forward pass, and at the end of a period. Also, one team may request a time out, and in that case play is stopped for one minute.

TOUCHBACK

When a punted ball goes over the receiving team's goal line and is grounded; or when a defensive player intercepts a forward pass behind his own goal line and decides not to try to run with the ball; or when a kicked ball hits the crossbar or goalpost and rolls into the end zone —these situations and others cause the football to be brought out to the twenty-yard line, from which point it is put in play.

TOUCHDOWN

An offensive team running with the ball, or successfully passing the ball over the other team's goal line, scores a touchdown, which counts for six points.

TRAP

A trap (sometimes also called "mousetrap") is a particular kind of block executed by an offensive lineman. The offensive lineman will allow his opponent to come across the line of scrimmage, then block him out to the side, so that the ball carrier can charge through the area left open by the defensive player.

TRIPLE THREAT

An offensive backfield player who can run with the ball, kick it for long distances, and pass very well is called "a triple threat man."

TRY FOR POINT

See Conversion.

TURN THE CORNER

On an end sweep, the ball carrier races behind the line of scrimmage, and when he gets outside his own end (between the offensive end position and the sidelines), he tries to "turn the corner" —that is, cut sharply upfield.

TWO ON ONE

See Double team.

UMPIRE

One of the officials at a football game. The umpire keeps a record of all time outs. He assists the referee in decisions involving a fumble, making sure the ball is securely in the possession of a player before awarding the ball to that player's team. The umpire also checks the equipment to make sure that no illegal shoes or other parts of a uniform are being used. He watches the conduct of the players on the line of scrimmage.

UNBALANCED LINE

As a rule, the offensive linemen line up as follows: the center in the middle of the line, a guard on either side of him, and a tackle beside each of the guards. Naturally, the ends are at the end of the line. Sometimes, however, two of the linemen will take up their stance out of their normal positions. For example, the two guards will be side-by-side, instead of being on either side of the center. That would make the line "unbalanced." The unbalanced line is perfectly legal.

SE   OT   OG   OG   OT   TE

UNBALANCED LINE

UNIT

Any team of eleven players is considered a "football unit." The defensive team is called "the defensive unit," the offensive team is the "offensive unit," the suicide squad is called the "kicking unit."

V PATTERN

A kind of pass pattern used by receivers. One or more pass receivers race away from the line of scrimmage, then slant toward the middle of the field. Suddenly, they slant back in the opposite direction, back toward the line of scrimmage. This kind of pattern looks like an upside-down V. When two pass receivers are both running the V pattern, they will cross paths. in order to confuse the defensive players trying to guard them.

WINGBACK

When the flanker back is stationed wide of the line, he is sometimes referred to as the "wingback."

WEAK SIDE

The side of the line that does *not* have the flanker back and tight end. Usually, it is the side of the offensive formation that has only a split end as receiver and no backfield man for support. However, it can happen that the flanker back and split end will take positions on the same side of the line. In that case the tight end area is called "the weak side."

YARDAGE

The ground that is gained, or lost, on plays from the line of scrimmage.

YARD CHAIN

A chain, which is exactly ten yards long, and is used to measure the progress of the ball as the offensive team tries to achieve a first down. Quite often, when the referee is not quite sure that the offensive team has gained the required ten yards, he (or the captain of the offensive or defensive team) will call for a measurement. The yard chains are brought out. One end is placed on the ground, exactly at the position the ball was when the series of downs started. Then the chain is stretched out as far as it will go. That is how the referee determines whether or not a first down has been achieved. (Sometimes, a tape is used instead of chain links.) Also called "measuring chain."

YARD LINE

Football fields are divided in such a way that every five yards there is a white line drawn from one sideline to the other. Between these lines are small "hashmarks," which are one yard apart. The white lines at five-yard intervals, and also the hashmarks, are considered yard lines.

YARDSTICKS

The poles to which the yard chain (or tape) is attached.

ZIG IN

A pass pattern run by receivers. To execute the zig in, the receiver races straight ahead a few yards, then cuts sharply toward the sideline. He continues in that direction for a few yards, then suddenly cuts toward the center of the field. His pattern forms a kind of letter "Z."

ZIG OUT

This is the exact opposite of zig in. The receiver starts out the same way, running straight ahead a few yards, and then cuts sharply toward the center of the field. He continues in that direction for a few yards, then cuts toward the sideline. Thus it is seen that "in" means "in toward

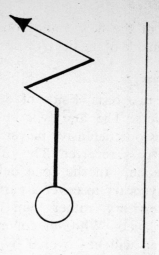

ZIG IN

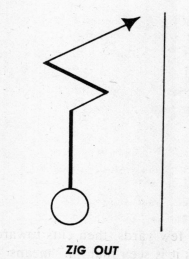

ZIG OUT

the center of the field," and "out" means "toward the outside of the field, or the sidelines."

ZONE DEFENSE

There are two basic kinds of defense against pass receivers. The first type is man-for-man. That means one defensive player is assigned to cover one pass receiver. The other basic defense is "zone." In the zone defense, the defensive players try to cover a particular area, a piece of territory, rather than the individual offensive players. Whoever comes into a zone defense area will be covered by the defensive player assigned to guard that piece of territory.

ABOUT THE AUTHOR
AND ILLUSTRATOR

HOWARD LISS was born in Brooklyn, New York. He has been a sports fan since the age of seven when he first saw the Brooklyn Dodgers play at Ebbets Field. When he went to school he would play baseball and football on Brooklyn's empty lots, continuing in high school and for his army team. After his discharge from the army, he began to write articles for children's periodicals. He has written more than fifty books, mostly in the area of sports. Some of his books on baseball and football have been written jointly with star athletes such as Y. A. Tittle, Yogi Berra, and Willie Mays. Mr. Liss finds it "a real labor of love to write sports books for young people." He has also written *Bowling Talk* and *Hockey Talk*, which are available in Archway Paperback editions.

FRANK ROBBINS was born in Boston, Massachusetts. He received two art scholarships by the time he was fourteen. He is now a versatile and creative artist who has drawn comic strips, exhibited in art shows, and illustrated for magazines and advertising.

Meet McGurk!

Got a mystery to solve? Just ask McGurk. He heads the McGurk Detective Organization, and he and his supersleuths—Wanda, Willie, Joey, and Brains Bellingham—can unravel just about anything! They've solved the puzzle of the ruthless bird killer, tracked down a missing newsboy, traced an <u>invisible</u> dog, and cracked the case of a mysterious robbery.

Can you solve these tricky cases?
Follow the clues and
match wits with master-mind McGurk!

The McGURK MYSTERIES, by E. W. Hildick,
illustrated by Iris Schweitzer:

ENTER DANIEL COHEN'S STRANGE WORLD OF GHOSTS, MONSTERS AND OTHER-WORLDLY BEINGS!

A Dog in a Million!

Pete's best friend is Mishmash—a big, friendly dog who thinks he's human. Mish sleeps in a bed, eats at the table, and takes bubble baths. He hops into cars hoping for rides, adopts an imaginary playmate, and even gives a party for his dog friends! Join Pete and Mishmash as they get mixed up in one hilarious adventure after another.

The MISHMASH books, by Molly Cone
illustrated by Leonard Shortall:

_____	56083	$1.50	MISHMASH
_____	43711	$1.75	MISHMASH AND THE SUBSTITUTE TEACHER
_____	43135	$1.75	MISHMASH AND THE SAUERKRAUT MYSTERY
_____	43682	$1.75	MISHMASH AND UNCLE LOOEY
_____	29936	$1.50	MISHMASH AND THE VENUS FLYTRAP

If your bookseller does not have the titles you want, you may order them by sending the retail price (plus 50¢ postage and handling—New York State and New York City residents please add appropriate sales tax) to: POCKET BOOKS, Dept. AMM, 1230 Avenue of the Americas, New York, N.Y. 10020. Send check or money order—no cash or C.O.D.s and be sure to include your name and address. Allow six weeks for delivery.

133

ARCHWAY PAPERBACKS from Pocket Books